Adapted and published in the United States in
1985 by Silver Burdett Company, Morristown,
N.J.

Library of Congress Cataloging in Publication Data

Williamson, Tom, 1944–
   The earth.

   (Understanding) (A Silver Burdett library selection)
   British ed. published under title: The science of the earth.
   Includes index.
   Summary: Discusses the structure, atmosphere, climate,
and features of our planet and examines its activity
and natural resources.
   1. Earth sciences—Juvenile literature.   2. Mines
and mineral resources—Juvenile literature.   [1. Earth]
I. Title.   II. Series.
QE29.W487   1985   550   85-40215

ISBN 0-382-09083-7

Designer
Julian Holland

Picture researcher
Stella Martin

Artists
Fred Anderson
Dan Escott
Sara Pooley

Editors
Penny Farrant
Miranda Smith

Photocredits:
Biofotos
British Petroleum
J Allan Cash Ltd
Martin Christidis
Bruce Coleman Ltd
C M Dixon
Michael Holford
Eric and David Hosking
Alan Hutchison Library
IMITOR
Institute of Geological Sciences
Mat Irvine
J M Jarvis
Dick Makin
Stella Martin
NASA
National History Photographic Agency
Picturepoint Ltd
Royal Astronomical Society
Science Photo Library
Shell
Spectrum Colour Library
Sperry Ltd
Tom Williamson
ZEFA

Understanding
The Earth

Tom Williamson

Silver Burdett Company

Morristown, New Jersey

Contents

◁ *The Iguacu waterfalls, Brazil.*

The Earth we live on

Our home in space, the Earth, is mostly made of iron, rocks, water and air. Living things, such as plants and animals are also part of the Earth. The force of gravity pulls all the parts of the Earth together. The heavy iron and rocks have been pulled into a vast ball, about 7,926.41 miles in diameter, and with a rather uneven surface. Although its surface is solid, volcanoes show that this rocky ball is hot and partly molten inside. Gravity has drawn the water into the hollows of the solid surface to form oceans while the air has been pulled into a thin layer around the solid Earth.

Life on Earth

Life exists anywhere on Earth which is not too hot, cold or dry, providing it receives enough sunlight and there is a supply of food. Tiny plants swarm in the sunlit surface waters of the oceans and bigger plants such as trees and grasses cover much of the land. Powered by the Sun, the plants work like factories turning water and air into food for themselves. They in turn are then eaten by animals.

▽ *The outer part of the Earth is made of layers of solid rocks. These layers have often been disturbed by ancient volcanoes and earthquakes. Over much of the Earth's surface the rocks are covered by a thin layer of soil. Green plants get some of their needs from this soil but to grow they also use gases from the atmosphere and energy from the Sun.*

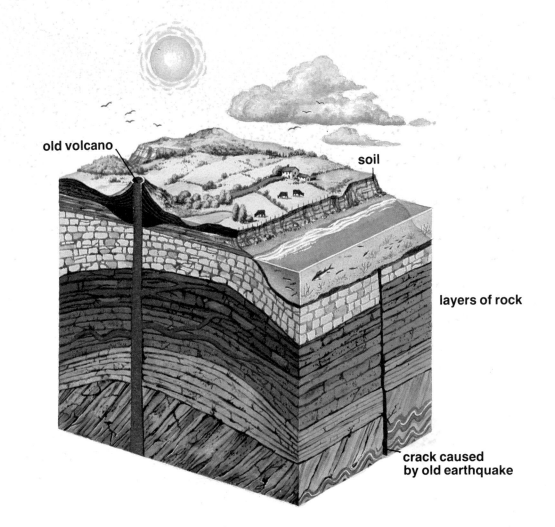

old volcano

soil

layers of rock

crack caused by old earthquake

▷ *The volcano Mount St Helens in Washington erupting in 1980. A huge cloud of hot gases and dust rose high into the atmosphere. Volcanoes show the inside of the Earth is hot.*

▽ *Rice being harvested in Japan. Green plants support all animal life on Earth. Plants provide food for animals to eat and oxygen gas for them to breathe.*

Over millions of years, living things have left their mark on the air, oceans and even on rocks. Thousands of millions of years ago, there was no oxygen gas in the air. Harmful rays from the Sun poured down on the land destroying any forms of life that dared to leave the safety of the sea.

Oxygen in the air

Slowly, plants developed in the sea and started to give off oxygen as they grew. Some of the oxygen dissolved in the seawater and some of it escaped into the air. Some of the oxygen in the air was turned into a gas, called ozone, which can absorb dangerous rays from the Sun. Because of the ozone shield, life could then develop on land as well as in the sea. As they developed, living things started to use the oxygen to breathe. Today, most living things in the sea, on land or in the air have to have oxygen to survive.

So many animals and plants have lived on the Earth that in places their remains have hardened into layers of rock. Shells of past sea creatures have turned into limestone while their bodies have turned into a thick oil that is used to make gasoline.

△ Seabirds such as these gannets are completely at home in the air of the Earth's atmosphere. The air supports the birds when they fly and the oxygen in it allows them and all other animals to breathe. The atmosphere protects the Earth from getting too hot or too cold and keeps out harmful rays.

◁ Oceans of water cover two thirds of our planet. Huge numbers of tiny plants live in the sunlit surface waters of the oceans. Like the plants on land, they use the Sun's energy to grow and so provide food for animal life such as these brightly colored fish and corals.

The spinning Earth

The Earth spins like a top, turning on an invisible axis which passes through the Earth's center and its North and South Poles. Unlike a top, the Earth will continue spinning for millions of years. A spinning top slows down because it touches the ground below and is surrounded by air. Because the Earth is surrounded by space and touches nothing, its spin hardly slows down at all.

◁ *This photograph of star tracks was taken over several minutes and shows how the stars seem to have moved. The tracks you can see here are all parts of large circles. The center of the circles is near the North Star which is above and to the right of this picture. People used to think the stars themselves moved in circles. Now we know that it is the Earth which really moves. As the Earth makes one turn every 24 hours, each star seems to make one circle in the sky.*

▽ *As the Earth spins, the stars of the Big Dipper seem to move around the North Star.*

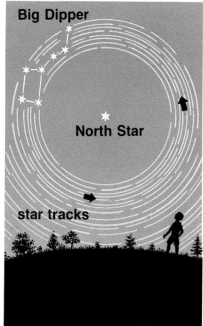

Big Dipper

North Star

star tracks

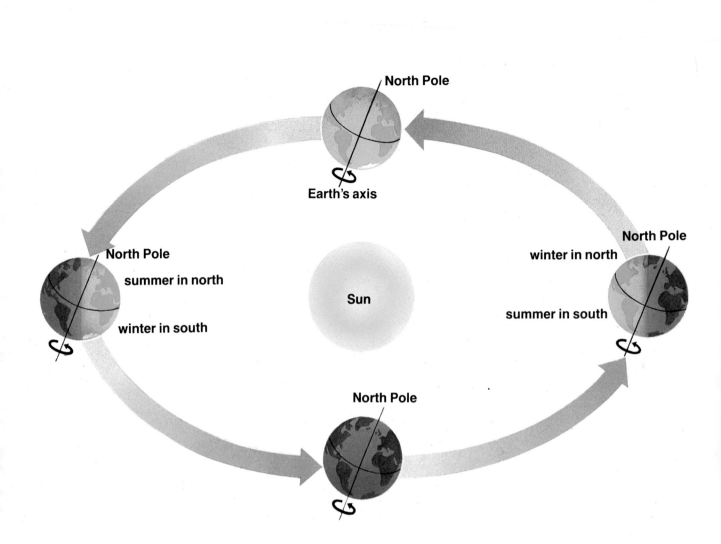

The Earth is like a huge spaceship rushing through space at about 60,000 miles per hour. If the Earth was traveling in a straight line, it would reach the distance of the nearest star to the Sun in about 40,000 years time. But the Earth is not able to move in a straight line because it is always being tugged at by the pull of the Sun's gravity. The Sun weighs as much as about 333,000 Earths and the pull of its gravity is very strong. It is this pull which stops the Earth from rushing off into space and keeps it circling around the Sun, in orbit.

The Earth and the Sun

We are lucky that the Earth spins fairly quickly as it travels around the Sun. If the Earth turned around very slowly like the planets Mercury or Venus, the Sun would heat its day side to boiling point while its night side would be frozen solid. As it is, most parts of the Earth never have time to get too hot by day or too cold by night.

The hottest parts of the Earth are those near the equator which face the Sun every day as the Earth turns around. Here it is hot by day and only slightly cooler by night. The coldest parts of the Earth are those around the North and South Poles which never face the Sun directly, even at midday.

△ The Earth we live on travels around one of the billions of stars in the universe. We call this star the Sun. As it travels around the Sun, the Earth also turns on its own axis. It turns around once every 24 hours but takes a whole year to journey right around the Sun. The Earth's axis is tilted as it moves around the Sun. The North Pole sometimes tilts towards the Sun and sometimes tilts away from the Sun. When the North Pole tilts towards the Sun it is summer in the northern part of the Earth. When the North Pole tilts away from the Sun, it is winter in the northern part of the Earth.

As the solid, rocky part of the Earth spins, the air and the oceans are dragged with it. Near the equator, the air and oceans are traveling very fast, like the water in the middle of a stream.

Currents of warm air and water

Farther away from the equator, the air and oceans move more slowly, like the water close to the banks of a stream. As a result, giant swirling currents of air and water form in the Earth's atmosphere and oceans, rather like the eddies in a stream.

These swirling currents help to carry warm air and water from the hot parts of the Earth near the equator towards the cold parts of the Earth near the North and South Poles. This warm air and water from the equator keeps most parts of the Earth warm enough for life to abound both in oceans and on land. Even near the North Pole itself there is life in the sea below the ice to provide food for animals such as seals and polar bears.

△ Earth, the blue and white planet, rising in the dark sky of the Moon. The part of the Earth we can see is bright because it is facing the Sun. Here it is day. The dark invisible part of the Earth is in night. You can just see the brown shapes of Earth's continents and the dark blue oceans beneath the clouds.

9

The atmosphere

We live at the bottom of a vast ocean of air — the atmosphere. There are many different gases in the air, all mixed together. Although the gases are light, they all feel the tug of the Earth's gravity and this stops most of them from drifting away into space. One gas, hydrogen, is so light that the Earth's gravity is not strong enough to keep it close to the Earth. So there is now almost no hydrogen in the air; any that there was has leaked away.

Other gases in the air

Some of the gases in the air, such as argon, carbon dioxide, neon, helium and ozone, are found in small amounts only. Water is present in the air as a gas called water vapor, but its amount varies from place to place. There is usually a great deal of water vapor in rainy places or near the sea but very little in dry places such as deserts.

The two most common gases in the atmosphere are nitrogen and oxygen. Both gases are important for life as most animals and plants need oxygen to breathe and they all need nitrogen to grow. Only a few living things can use the nitrogen in the air directly. Most plants get it from the soil while animals get it by eating plants or other animals.

Imagine being pulled up into the air by a balloon filled with hydrogen or helium. Because these gases are lighter than the air around, the balloon will rise in the air just as an air bubble rises in a pool of water. As you rise higher and higher, it gets colder and colder. Then you may suddenly find that it gets very misty and you can no longer see the ground. This means that you are passing through a cloud.

Clouds are made of water droplets or ice crystals that are so tiny that they float in the air. They usually form when water vapor rises into the air above and is cooled. As the balloon carries you higher, the wind will probably get stronger. If you are unlucky, the balloon might be carried into a storm, with very strong winds and heavy rain or snow.

The stratosphere

If the balloon manages to rise high above the storm clouds, to six miles or more above the ground, you will see a great change. The sky will be blue and all the clouds will lie beneath you. You will have reached an upper layer of the atmosphere called the stratosphere. Here it is bitterly cold and the air is so thin that you will need extra oxygen to breathe. Jetplanes usually fly in the stratosphere because they save fuel by flying through the thinner air. As your balloon rises in the stratosphere it will gradually slow down as the air around gets thinner and thinner. It will stop rising altogether when the air becomes so thin that it is just as light as your balloon.

△ The Sun's heat and the spin of the Earth stir the Earth's atmosphere into endless motion. This produces weather and storms. The swirling clouds of a hurricane can be seen here.

◁ Clouds form when a gas called water vapor cools. When it cools, the vapor turns to liquid water or solid ice. Clouds consist of tiny droplets of water or crystals of ice floating in the air.

▷ This welder is using oxygen gas to help make a hot flame. Oxygen is the second most common gas in the air.

As air is cooled, some of the water vapor in it turns into liquid water. When it gets colder, the water turns to ice and some of the water vapor left in the air also turns into ice. As air is cooled further, more and more water vapor turns into ice.

In the coldest places on Earth there is only a tiny amount of water vapor left in the air because most of it has already changed into ice. If air is cooled below the temperature of these very cold places, the carbon dioxide gas in it changes into a solid called "dry ice." There is dry ice on the planet Mars, which is very cold because it is much farther from the Sun than the Earth is.

Useful gases

When air is cooled even further, the gases oxygen, argon and nitrogen turn into liquids, one by one. These gases have many uses and so there are factories which cool air to produce them. The liquid gases are separated from each other and kept in strong steel cylinders.

Oxygen is used in the welding of metals, to help sick people breathe, to make the fuel burn in rockets and in hundreds of other ways. Among other things, argon is used to fill lamp bulbs and in metal working.

The biggest use of nitrogen is in the making of ammonia, which is a very useful gas. A mixture of nitrogen and hydrogen is heated and squeezed until the two gases join to form ammonia. The main use for ammonia is as a fertilizer for plants. The nitrogen in it helps the plants to grow.

△ Here you can see cotton being sprayed with a fertilizer containing nitrogen. Nitrogen is the most common gas in the Earth's atmosphere. But plants cannot usually use the nitrogen in the air directly. So they are given it in the form of fertilizers such as ammonia.

◁ Carbon dioxide is the gas that bubbles out of sodas like the one this boy has. It is also found in small quantities in the atmosphere. Plants use carbon dioxide and water to grow.

The water cycle

Wherever there is liquid water, there is also some water vapor in the air around. Water vapor is made of the same tiny particles that make up liquid water. But in the vapor the water particles are much farther apart than in liquid water. The water vapor particles mix with the particles of the other gases in the air.

The effect of the Sun's heat

When liquid water is heated, some tiny water particles escape from the liquid, adding to the water vapor already in the air. This is what happens when water in the sea or a lake is heated by the Sun. At the same time, the Sun's heat causes the mixture of water vapor and other gases in the air to expand. As they expand, the water vapor and other gases become lighter than the colder air above. The heated water vapor and other gases rise into the colder air, in the same way as a balloon filled with a light gas rises in the atmosphere.

▽*When the Sun shines on a sea or lake, water turns into water vapor. As the vapor rises it cools and this turns it into tiny water droplets or ice crystals. These form clouds in the atmosphere. The tiny droplets or crystals may then join together to form larger water drops or snow flakes. They fall to the ground as rain or snow. The water from the rain or melted snow then flows back to the sea in rivers or underground.*

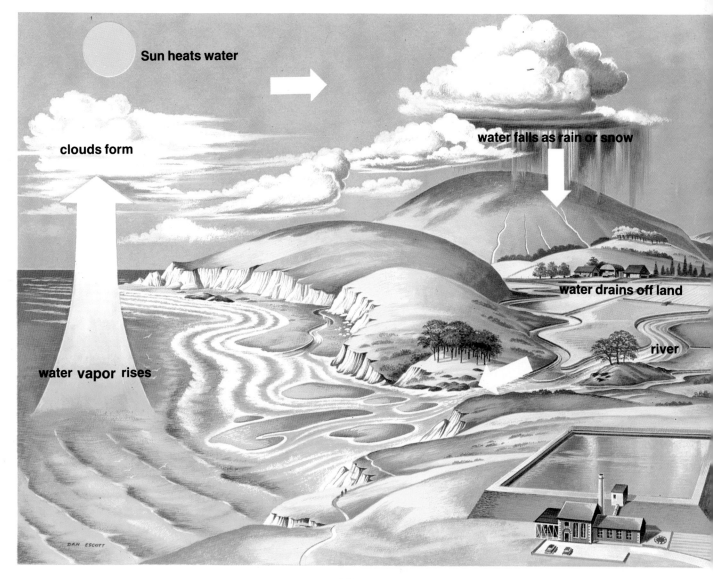

13

◁ When rain falls high in the mountains, Earth's gravity pulls it downward. As the streams of water flow downhill, they pick up small pieces of rock on the way. At the bottom of a waterfall like this, the water may be traveling with the speed of a fast car. The force of the water and bits of rock it is carrying will in the end wear away a huge cleft in the cliff.

◁ Trees take part in the water cycle. They suck up water from the ground through their roots. Some of this water is used to help them grow but some is passed into their leaves and turns into water vapor. This rises to help form clouds and rain. So if trees are cut down, less water vapor rises in the air and less rain may fall. Many places now have less rain than before because people have cut down trees.

All clouds contain water, either as tiny droplets of liquid water or as tiny crystals of ice. The droplets or ice crystals are so small that they float in the air. Sometimes the droplets or crystals grow into bigger rain drops or snow flakes. Because this makes them heavier they are pulled downward by the Earth's gravity and fall to the ground as rain or snow.

Glaciers

What happens next depends on the temperature. If the temperature stays below the freezing point of water, the snow flakes do not melt. Instead, they pile up to form a layer of snow. If the snow piles up year after year, the bottom layers eventually turn to ice. When a large amount of this kind of ice forms, it is called a glacier. Glaciers form on lands near the North and South Poles and on high mountains. The glacier ice is pulled downward by the Earth's gravity and creeps very slowly towards the sea.

Water drains off the land

If the temperature rises above the freezing point of water, any snow that falls melts. Some of the water from the melted snow or rain trickles along the ground surface until it finds its way into a stream or river. It then flows downhill towards the sea. Some of the rainwater soaks into the soil and is then taken up by plants through their roots.

Some water soaks right through the soil into cracks in the rocks below. Rainwater is slightly acidic, like a soda, because the water drops have absorbed some carbon dioxide gas from the air. As it soaks down into the cracks, the acid rainwater slowly dissolves away parts of any limestone rocks that may be there. In this way, long caves are formed. The rainwater flows downhill along the bottom of the cave system towards the sea as an underground stream.

△ This limestone cave was formed by rainwater flowing underground towards the sea. People who explore caves like this are called "spelunkers."

Experiment!

Heat some water in a kettle. As it gets hotter the water gives off invisible vapor.

The invisible vapor will turn into water when it hits a cold surface such as a window.

The mopped-up water will start to flow back to the sea from the sink.

Winds and weather

You can find out quite a lot about the air around you by looking and feeling. It is easy to see if there are any clouds in the sky and if it is raining or not. You can feel whether the air is hot or cold and if there is a lot of water vapor in the air you may feel sticky. If the air is moving past you, you can feel it as a wind. You can even tell where the wind is coming from by turning around until it blows in your face. In these different ways, you can keep a record of how the weather changes from day to day, from week to week, and from month to month.

Weather instruments

There are several instruments you can use to find out more about the weather. A thermometer tells you not only whether it is hot or cold, but how hot it is or how cold it is. Another instrument called a barometer tells you something about the weather that you cannot usually feel at all. It tells you whether the pressure of the air is high or low.

When the pressure gets higher, the air squeezes a metal box inside the barometer and turns the needle to the right. When the air pressure gets lower, the metal box can expand again and this turns the needle to the left. So by keeping a record of the position of the barometer needle you can see how the pressure changes from day to day.

▽ Although air is light, it still has weight. At sea level the full weight of all the air in Earth's atmosphere is above you. The air presses in on each square centimeter of your body with the force of a one kilogram weight. If you climb a mountain, there will be less air above you and so the pressure will be lower. At the top of a high mountain the air pressure may be only half as much as it is at sea level. Even at the same height, pressure varies from place to place and from day to day. You can see how pressure changes from the movement of the needle of a barometer.

6000 meters above sea level
pressure = 0.5 kilogram per square centimeter

0.5 kg

sea level
pressure = 1 kilogram per square centimeter

0.5 kg
0.5 kg

If you keep a barometer record, you may notice that on sunny days the air pressure is usually high. On rainy days you may find that the pressure is usually low. It is easy to understand this if you remember how the water cycle works to give clouds and rain.

Clouds and rain form when warm air and water vapor rise, like a balloon filled with hot air. When the air rises, this leaves less air below and the pressure falls. So if your barometer shows that pressure is falling, clouds and rain may be coming.

In some parts of the world the pressure is usually low and in other parts it is usually high. In mountains and highlands the pressure is low because there is less air above. Pressure is usually low near the equator, where hot air rises bringing clouds and rain. But pressure is usually high in desert areas, where air sinks rather than rises.

△ Balloons filled with hot air rise in the atmosphere. This is because when air is heated, it expands and becomes lighter than the cold air around.

▷ The sails of this boat are being filled by wind. Winds are caused when air heated by the Sun rises, like a hot air balloon. As the pressure falls, cold air rushes in to take the place of the warmer air. We feel the moving air as wind.

Winds are affected by the spin of the Earth. The spin causes winds to spiral in towards areas of low pressure. These spiraling winds usually bring clouds and rain. Near the equator where the Sun heats the sea very strongly, fierce storms called hurricanes are produced. These big rain storms are also called typhoons or cyclones. They can cover an area as much as 300 miles across and the winds can blow at over 180 miles per hour.

As well as hurricanes, there are other smaller spiraling storms such as tornadoes and whirlwinds. Tornadoes are very fierce whirlwinds that form on land. The pressure inside a tornado is so low that anything in its way gets sucked up.

Experiment!

Fix one blown up balloon and another not, onto a tube. Squeeze the tube.

Stop squeezing. Air will rush into the balloon in which the pressure is lower.

The Earth's different climates

If you keep a weather record for several years, you may find the same kind of weather occurs at the same time each year. Keep a month by month check on how it changes.

In cold, rainy parts of the world it will probably be cold in winter, with some snow and rain. In the spring it will get warmer but may still be quite wet. The summer months will probably be the driest with some hot spells. This is the pattern of weather in the British Isles. The pressure is often low and there are clouds and rain throughout the year.

In other parts of the world, the climate is quite different. In the zone of hot, rainy climates near the equator, every day is warm or hot and the pressure is usually low. The Sun's heat sets the water cycle going strongly, often giving clouds and rain later in the day. Farther away from the equator lie two zones of very dry climates. Here the air pressure is usually high and rain is very rare.

Polar weather

Near the Earth's poles, the weather is nearly always cold because the Sun's heating is weak. In some parts of this zone, such as northern Canada, the temperature rises above freezing in the summer. In the polar zone the pressure is usually high and there is only a little snow.

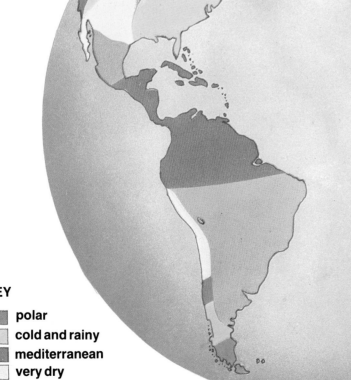

KEY

- polar
- cold and rainy
- mediterranean
- very dry
- savannah
- hot and rainy

△ The climate is very cold near the poles because these areas receive little heat from the Sun. The Arctic Ocean, around the North Pole, is covered by ice. But fish live in the warmer water below and provide food for seals and polar bears.

△ The grasslands of East Africa have long dry periods. Trees are scattered thinly and are able to withstand droughts. Grasslands like this are called savannahs. Large areas of the African savannahs have been turned into game reserves.

◁ This is Brixham, a seaside resort in the south west of the British Isles. The islands lie in the belt of cold and rainy climates. But they are surrounded by sea and lie in the path of a warm ocean current called the Gulf Stream. The current's warming effect keeps the winters mild, with little snow.

▷ The Rocky Mountains lie in the band of cold, rainy climates. The mountains here are far from the sea and the land heats up quickly in the summer and cools quickly in the winter.

△ The Sahara desert in Africa has a very dry climate. The air pressure is usually high and there is little rain.

▷ The rainforests of South America lie in the band of hot, rainy climates. Each day the Sun's heating is strong, causing moist air to rise. Clouds quickly form and there is soon a downpour of rain. The hot, moist climate is ideal for animals such as this iguana.

The frozen world

Near the poles of the Earth and high up in mountains the temperature is usually below the freezing point of water. Water cannot then be liquid so it has to be a solid or a vapor. In solid water, or ice, the tiny particles of water cannot move and are arranged in a fixed pattern. You can see this pattern in the shapes of ice crystals that make up snowflakes.

Summer melting

In some places near the poles, such as northern Canada and northern Siberia, most of the water in the ground stays frozen all year. Only the ice in the top layer of the ground melts in the summer. When the ice melts, the water takes up less space than the ice did, so the ground collapses and sinks down slightly. Because it is so unstable it is difficult to build houses and roads on ground like this. Houses are sometimes built on stilts stuck firmly in the layer of ground that is always frozen so the house is not affected when the ice melts.

Ice sheets

In other places near the poles, such as Antarctica and Greenland, the ground is buried beneath thick sheets of ice. In Antarctica the ice is more than two miles thick in places and the center of the Greenland ice sheet is more than one mile thick. Ice sheets form over thousands of years as layers of snow pile up and slowly turn into ice.

▷ *This boulder was carried here by ice. Glaciers tear off lumps from the rock beneath as they creep towards the sea. The lumps of rock become stuck in the ice and are carried along with the glacier. When the ice melts the rocks are left stranded like this.*

▽ *Floating icebergs are huge pieces of ice that have broken away from glaciers. Some icebergs are more than six miles long. They break off when the glacier reaches the sea. The ice floats because it is lighter than water.*

Ice sheets and glaciers are pulled downward by the Earth's gravity and creep slowly towards the sea. The ice usually moves no more than a few yards each day. If the glacier starts in a mountain range outside the polar regions, more and more ice will melt as it creeps down the valley. In the end all the ice will melt and the water will continue its journey to the sea as a stream.

If the glacier or ice sheet is in the polar region, the ice will stay frozen all the way to the sea. When it reaches the shore, it may be pushed out to sea as a floating shelf. Pieces of the shelf then break off as icebergs. Because ice is slightly lighter than seawater, icebergs float, but only just. Most of the iceberg is hidden below the surface of the sea.

Past Ice Ages

In parts of Europe and North America you can sometimes see large boulders that seem to have been dropped down from above. These boulders were carried to these places by ice sheets or glaciers during past Ice Ages, and were left behind when the ice melted. The Ice Ages were times when the Earth's climate was colder than it is now. There were huge ice sheets in North America and Europe as well as Antarctica and Greenland. Because more of the Earth's water was ice, there was less water in the oceans and the sea level was lower than it is today.

△ Glaciers are rivers of ice. They form in mountains or other cold places where snow piles up year after year. After many years, the snow gets squashed and turns into ice. The ice moves slowly downhill toward the sea where huge lumps may break off to form floating icebergs.

sea level if all the world's ice melted

sea level now

When the ice melts

New York would look like this if the Earth's temperature rose slightly so that all the world's ice suddenly melted. The water from melted glaciers would flow into the sea and the extra water would cause the level of the sea to rise by more than 150 feet. Many low lying lands would be flooded.

Another Ice Age

The English Channel might look like this in an Ice Age because the sea level would drop. In an Ice Age snow would pile up to form glaciers instead of melting and so less water would flow into the sea. Sea level would fall and many shallow seas like the Channel would become dry land. This is what happened during the last Ice Age which was at its coldest about 18,000 years ago. A huge ice sheet then covered most of northern Europe. After about 10,000 years ago the ice sheets melted rapidly and the sea level got higher and higher. By about 7,000 years ago the sea level was high enough to flood the Channel and make Britain an island.

Planet water

Over most of the Earth's surface, the temperature is usually above the freezing point of water. Water cannot then be solid so it has to be a liquid or a vapor. Most of the Earth's water is liquid and most of this liquid has been pulled by gravity into the lowest parts of the Earth. These parts are the ocean basins and we call the water that fills them oceans or seas. The ocean basins are usually about two miles deep but some places in them are as much as six miles below sea level.

▽ Waves breaking on the volcanic rocks of Lanzarote, an island in the Atlantic Ocean. Winds stir the ocean's surface into waves which break as they reach shallow water near the shore.

The water in the top layer of the oceans is dragged along by the wind above. In places where the wind usually blows in the same direction, the water also flows in this direction as an ocean current.

Some currents carry warm water from the equator toward the poles. Other currents carry cold water from the poles toward the equator.

Warm and cold currents

The British Isles and western Europe lie in the path of a warm current called the Gulf Stream. The Galapagos Islands off the coast of South America lie in the path of a cold current called the Humboldt Current.

The tiny particles of water that take part in the water cycle spend most of their time in the oceans. They spend only a small part of their time in the atmosphere and in rivers, streams or underground water. As the tiny water particles travel back to the sea they carry with them minute particles of various materials dissolved from air, soil and rocks. These salty materials from the land end up in the sea.

Underwater hot springs in the middle of the oceans also add salty material to the sea. Once in the sea, all these tiny particles of salty materials stay there. They are too heavy to escape from the sea's surface into the air.

High tide
Tides are caused by the pull of the Moon's gravity and the Sun's gravity on the water in the oceans. The pull draws the water upward in places. Where this happens there is a high tide. At high tide on a rocky coast like this the waves beat strongly against the cliffs, slowly wearing them away.

Low tide
This is the same stretch of coast as the one above, at low tide. The water has been pulled away by the Sun and Moon's gravity to another part of the world, where it is high tide. The difference in height between tides is usually small on islands where the water gets deep quickly. It is greater on coasts where the sea is shallow.

Salt from the Earth's seas is very useful. It is used to season and preserve food and to make useful chemicals. Some salt is obtained from seawater directly. In sunny climates, seawater is allowed to flow into shallow pools close to the sea called salt pans. The Sun's heat causes all the water in the pans to turn into vapor until a time is reached when the seawater can no longer hold all the salty material in solution.

Some of the salty material then collects on the bottom of the pan as very small white crystals. Usually the first crystals to form are a substance called calcium carbonate. Then the crystals of common salt form. When all the water has turned into vapor, a white mixture of common salt and other salty materials is left behind. Salt is also mined from layers formed in some places when seas evaporated in the past.

△ During storms, waves break against these cliffs with great force. They have slowly worn away the base of the cliff so that the top overhangs.

△ Sea creatures such as the whelk build their shells from the calcium carbonate dissolved in seawater. Underground water and water in rivers and streams dissolves some of the calcium carbonate and other salty materials in rocks and soils. This water then flows into the sea carrying the dissolved materials with it. All the calcium carbonate and salty material then stays in the sea.

Experiment!

Pour some seawater into a shallow dish. The water will slowly evaporate.

When all the water has gone white crystals of salty materials will remain.

27

The living seas

For tiny plants, life in the sea is very easy. There are lots of dissolved materials in the seawater which they can use to help them grow. In the top layer of water there is plenty of sunlight to give them energy. The hot springs on the ocean floor also provide energy for some of them.

The smallest plants and animals

The tiny plants that live in the sea do not need roots and leaves like plants on land. So they can be very small and simple. Some of them live in tiny shells. Many of these plants just drift around until they die or are eaten by an animal. Many of the animals that drift or swim around in the sea, eating the tiny plants, are also very small. There are lots of minute shrimp-like creatures, tiny animals with shells, and also the young of larger creatures like jellyfish.

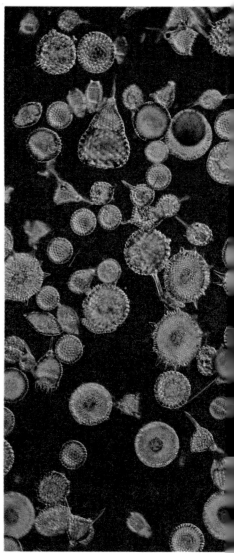

△ Tiny shells like these pile up on the floor of the deep ocean. They once belonged to the very small animals and plants that lived in the top layer of the sea.

◁ These corals live in the Red Sea. Coral polyps are animals with stinging tentacles, rather like sea anemones. They feed on tiny plants and animals drifting through the water.

Many of the plants and animals that live in the top layer of sea, where sunlight penetrates, have shells or hard parts. Those that live far away from the land, where the water is deep, usually have tiny shells. When they die, the shells drop slowly to the bottom and pile up, like snow, on the ocean floor. Those that live in shallow water close to the shore often have big shells or build large homes for themselves.

How sea animals protect themselves

Animals like whelks, oysters, cowries and clams have big shells while many corals live in large stony structures. Starfish and sea lilies or crinoids build an armor of plates around themselves. All the animals and plants build their shells or hard parts from the salty materials dissolved in the seawater. Most of them use calcium carbonate as a building material, but some use silica, which is the material of which sand is made.

△ *Sea lilies or crinoids are animals, not plants. They belong to the same family of animals as starfish and sea urchins. A crinoid attaches itself to a rock on the seabed. It feeds on animals and plants in the water around it.*

After a shell-owning animal has died, its shell may be washed up on a beach by tides, currents and waves. On some beaches you can often find many different shells which have been washed up in this way. In places near the equator, where the water is always warm, the beach may be fringed by a coral reef.

Coral reefs

Reefs are mainly built by animals called coral polyps. Each polyp lives in a stony cup made of calcium carbonate. As young polyps grow out from older ones, they too build their own stony cups. As more and more young polyps grow at the top and old ones die at the bottom, a branching stony structure grows upward toward the surface of the sea. A coral reef is made up of countless numbers of these corals, the young polyps living at the top of a huge stony mass that housed their ancestors.

Just as tiny shells pile up on the deep ocean floor, bigger shells and remains of corals and crinoids sometimes pile up in shallow waters close to the shore. Where the sea floor has sunk over millions of years, thick piles of squashed shelly materials have formed. Where the sea floor has been pushed up again, the old squashed corals, shells and crinoids can be seen on dry land as fossils in limestone.

△ *These fossil corals were found in England. They are millions of years old. This type of coral lives in warm seas, like the Red Sea today, so these fossils show that England was once warmer and covered by water. Similar fossils can be found in many other parts of the world.*

▷ *A sea otter enjoys a meal of squid. The squid's strong tentacles have proved no match for the otter's sharp teeth. The squid itself is a hunter, catching prey such as lobsters and crabs.*

Volcanoes

A volcano is a place where a mixture of hot molten rock and dissolved gases escapes from inside the Earth. When this mixture, which is called magma, reaches the surface the gas bubbles out of the liquid as it does when you open a bottle or can of soda.

Sometimes the gas escapes easily and the volcano may pour out the hot molten rock as a flow of lava. The hot lava runs downhill away from the mouth of the volcano, cooling and turning solid as it flows. Lava eruptions like this often happen in Hawaii.

Volcanic explosions

Sometimes the gases cannot escape so easily. They may build up inside the volcano until there is a huge explosion and the gases burst out with small bits of molten lava. The cloud of hot gases from the volcano, tiny bits of cooling lava and hot air rises high into the atmosphere. When the mixture cools and stops rising, the bits of cooling lava fall to the ground as volcanic ash or pumice. This is what happened when the Thera volcano, in the Mediterranean Sea, erupted in about 1600 BC and when Mount St Helens, Washington, erupted in 1980.

▽ *A volcanic eruption on the island of Hawaii. Here the hot molten rock is runny, like water, and some of it shoots into the air like a fountain. The gas escapes from the runny lava quite easily and so there are no big explosions. The lava flows quickly downhill from the mouth of the volcano. Sometimes it may cover more than 30 miles before it becomes solid.*

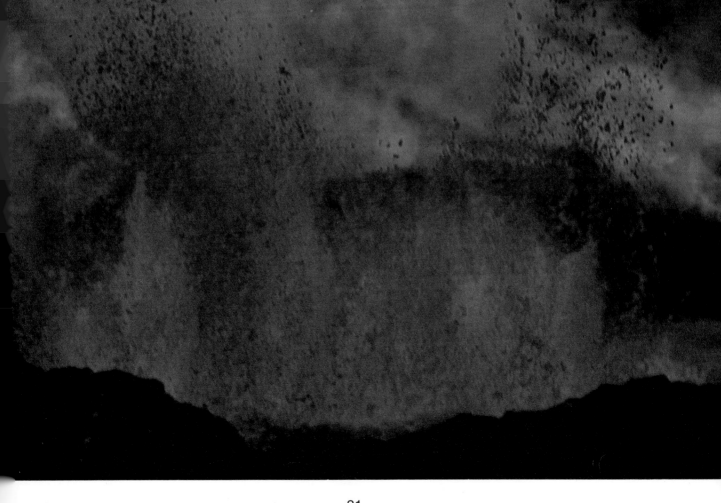

◁ This town is built on cliffs of pumice and ash that shot out from the Thera volcano. The pressure built up inside the volcano until there was a vast explosion and a hot cloud of gases and pieces of gassy lava rose high into the atmosphere. As it tried to escape, the gas blew the lava into pieces of a light frothy rock called pumice. This fell back to the ground and piled up in layers. So much pumice escaped from below the ground that nothing was left to hold up the center of the volcano. It sank into the sea leaving these cliffs behind.

▷ Olympus Mons on the planet Mars is the largest known volcano. It is about 360 miles across and the big crater at the top is about 40 miles wide. Olympus Mons is the same shape as the Mauna Loa volcano on Earth. Both have gentle slopes and are shaped rather like giant upturned saucers. These volcanoes are made of thousands of flows of runny lava, piled one on top of each other.

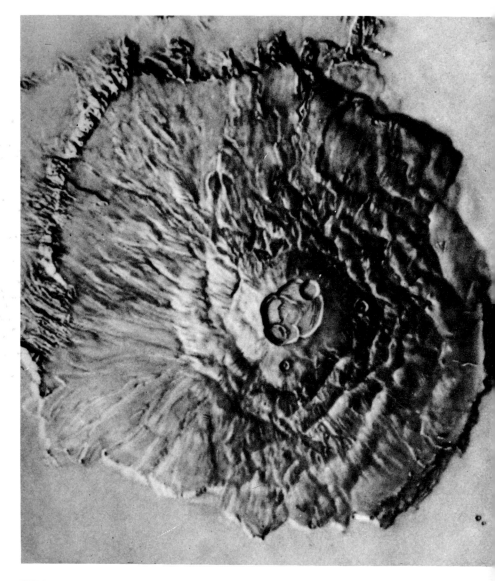

◁ Mount St Helens volcano, in Washington, usually throws out or emits pumice, ash or pasty lava. These pile up around the volcano's mouth to give it steep slopes. Volcanoes like Mount St Helens may only erupt once every hundred years or so. In March and April of 1980, Mount St Helens started to emit steam and ash and then began to bulge. Then, on May 18, 1980, a landslide let the gas and lava inside the mountain escape. A vast cloud of hot gas, pumice and ash burst out. Most of the people who had stayed near the volcano were killed.

Experiment!

Make your own volcanic explosion! Shake a bottle of soda until it bubbles.

When you open it gas and soda will burst out like an erupting volcano.

Volcanic rocks

Volcanoes produce several kinds of lava and ash. Underwater volcanoes on the ocean floor and volcanoes on islands in the centers of oceans usually pour out a fairly dark lava called basalt.

Volcanoes near the edges of continents and oceans often emit paler lavas. These volcanoes sometimes explode violently when gas pressure builds up inside them, and often produce ash or pumice. The few volcanoes that are well inside continents usually produce basalt. Most kinds of volcanic ash and lava eventually turn into very fertile soils. So people often farm close to volcanoes, even though they may be dangerous.

If you look closely at a piece of lava, you may see one or two big crystals in a mass of tiny crystals. The small crystals formed when the hot liquid magma came out of the volcano and cooled quickly to solid. Because it cooled so quickly, there was no time for the crystals to grow big. The big crystals grew beforehand when the magma cooled very slowly in an underground chamber.

Plutonic rocks

In many parts of the world you can find rocks that are made up of big crystals only. These rocks formed millions of years ago when hot magma cooled many miles underground.

Over millions of years, the rocks above slowly crumbled away until nothing remained above and the rocks with big crystals were left at the surface. Rocks formed in this way are called plutonic rocks after Pluto, the Greek god of the underworld. Many plutonic rocks are pale in color and you can see clear crystals of quartz and white or pink crystals of feldspar in them. Such rocks are granites.

▷ *Edinburgh, Scotland, may have looked like this about 300 million years ago. The sea then covered this part of Scotland. A big volcano rose from the sea floor with its summit above sea level. Around the big volcano were several little ones. The molten lava from the volcanoes cooled quickly to form dark rocks with tiny crystals called basalt. The lava in the pipes of the volcanoes also cooled to form basalt. The basalt rocks from the pipes of the old volcanoes now form the hills of Edinburgh.*

▷ These granite rocks were once molten. The molten rock did not rise to the surface and form a volcano. Instead it cooled many miles underground. Large crystals grew in the hot liquid as it slowly cooled. In the end all the liquid became solid granite. Over millions of years the water cycle slowly wore away the rocks above so the granite is now at the surface. The rocks around a body of granite often wear away faster than the granite itself. The granite then sticks up as a rocky hill.

◁ This strange tower of rock in France is the pipe which once took molten rock and gas to the top of a volcano. After the supply of molten rock and gas ran out, the volcano started to crumble away. In the end only the solid rock in the pipe was left. If you dug down and followed the pipe many miles into the ground, you would probably find that it would pass into a large mass of dark rock with big crystals. This would have once been the chamber that fed the volcano with hot magma.

△ This famous palace in Spain, the Escorial, is built of granite. Because granite is hard, pleasant to look at and does not wear away easily, it has been used a great deal as a building stone, particularly for churches, castles and palaces. Granite is also often used for statues and as curb stones for pavements.

▷ This is a piece of granite. The pink and white crystals you can see are feldspar, the gray ones are quartz and the dark flaky crystals are mica.

Granites sometimes also contain crystals with useful metals in them such as tin, tungsten or uranium. These are called ore minerals. Sometimes the ore minerals are scattered through the granite. Sometimes you can find them in cracks which cut through the granite and the rocks around. To get them miners sink deep holes into the ground and then tunnel sideways until they reach a crack with ore minerals.

Erosion and sedimentary rocks

The weather and the water cycle cause granite, lava and other rocks to slowly crumble away. In cold places, rainwater may soak into cracks in the rock and then freeze. Ice needs more space than water, so the water pushes the cracks open as it freezes. In the end pieces of rock split off.

Rainwater also slowly dissolves limestone and changes feldspar and mica crystals in granite to clay particles. Streams and glaciers then carry the bits of rock, quartz crystals and clay particles downhill.

△ *These mountains in Switzerland are being slowly worn down by glaciers and streams. The rocks crumble away as water soaks into cracks and then freezes. The small pieces of rock are picked up by the ice or water and carried toward the sea.*

◁ *This huge statue in Egypt was carved more than two thousand years ago. Heating by day, cooling by night, wind, sandstorms and rain have caused the rock to slowly crumble away.*

◁ These layers of eroded limestone and sandstone in Utah were formed long ago when the area was under the sea. Layers of shells piled up on the sea floor and sand was brought into the area by rivers. Over millions of years the layers of shells were squashed to form limestone and the layers of sand were squashed to form sandstone. Layered rocks of this kind are called sedimentary rocks. After millions more years, the layers were pushed above sea level and now they are being eroded. Freezing and thawing of ice and water are breaking up the sandstone layers while rainwater is dissolving the limestone away. The broken up pieces of rock are piling up below.

Pieces of rock, quartz crystals and tiny clay particles are carried downhill by water or ice. The corners are rubbed off the pieces of rock and quartz crystals as they bump into each other. They become smaller and rounder and end up as grains of sand. If they reach the coast, the sand grains may pile up on beaches and in shallow waters.

In other parts of the sea floor, clay particles or shells made of calcium carbonate may pile up. Where the sea floor has sunk over millions of years, thick layers of sand, clay or shells have formed. The sand has stuck together to form sandstone while the clay has been squeezed into shale and the shells into limestone. Where the sea floor has been pushed up again, the sandstone, shale or limestone can be seen on land.

△ Sand dunes in the Sahara desert in Africa. Dunes like these may turn into sandstone in millions of years time.

▷ This sandstone was formed in a desert millions of years ago. The layers cutting across each other are the slopes of the old sand dunes. When rocks such as granite crumble away, the quartz crystals in them are released. They are then carried by rivers or the wind to low areas such as the seashore or deserts. As the grains bump into each other, their corners are rubbed off and they get smaller and rounder.

Experiment!

Build a little mountain of sand and small pebbles, all mixed together.

Pour on water. Little rivers will form and carry the sand away.

Earthquakes and faulting

Each year there are earthquakes in some parts of the world. The ground shakes fiercely, landslides may be started and sometimes huge cracks open up in the surface.

Many earthquakes happen under the sea or in deserted areas. These earthquakes are usually harmless to people. But when a big earthquake happens in an area with cities and towns, many people may be killed and injured as the buildings fall down.

Some types of buildings are safer than others. Wooden buildings or those with strong steel frames are less likely to fall down than those made of bricks or stones. Houses built on solid rocks like granite are usually safer than those built on clay or sands.

Predicting earthquakes

If people could tell when a earthquake was coming, many lives could be saved. Sometimes there are signs before a big quake, such as small earthquake shocks or changes in the level of water in wells. Sometimes animals behave strangely. In places where earthquakes often happen, scientists try to look out for signs like these. Then if a big quake seems likely, people can be warned of it.

◁ These buildings in California collapsed during an earthquake. As the ground shook, a huge crack opened up in the road. Earthquakes can bring disaster when they hit towns or cities. People may be hurt, roads broken up, water and electricity supplies cut off and houses and hospitals destroyed.

▷ Most earthquakes happen in narrow belts that wind across the Earth. Japan, California and countries around the Mediterranean Sea all lie in earthquake zones like this. Earthquake belts mark the borders between large areas called plates. There are few earthquakes in the centers of the plates, away from their edges. This is because quakes are caused by movement between the plates.

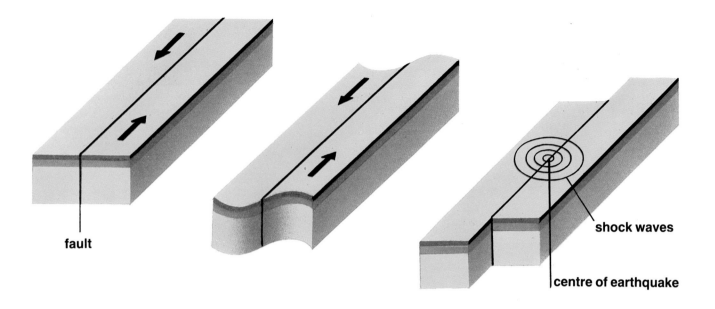

fault

shock waves

centre of earthquake

△ Earthquakes happen when there is a movement between two blocks of land, along a huge crack called a fault. Before the earthquake the blocks stick together. They bend but cannot move. Then suddenly they slip and shock waves spead out, shaking the ground fiercely. The shaking is greatest near the fault and more gentle farther out. The strength of the earthquake tremors can be measured with instruments called seismographs.

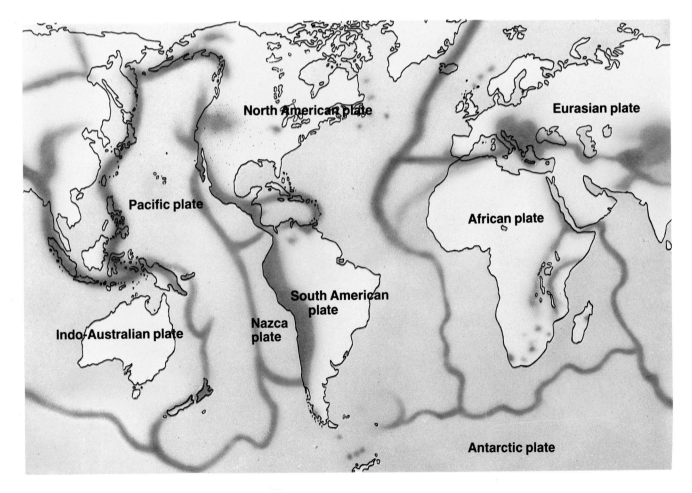

North American plate

Eurasian plate

Pacific plate

African plate

South American plate

Nazca plate

Indo-Australian plate

Antarctic plate

Seismographs

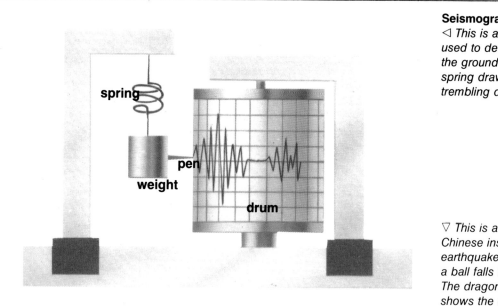

◁ This is a modern seismograph, used to detect earthquakes. When the ground shakes, a pen on a spring draws a wavy line on the trembling drum.

spring

pen

weight

drum

▽ This is a model of an old Chinese instrument for detecting earthquakes. If the ground shakes, a ball falls from a dragon's mouth. The dragon that loses its ball shows the direction that the earthquake is coming from.

Living on rafts

Using seismographs, scientists can find out how the Earth's plates move when earthquakes happen. In some places two plates are slowly slipping past each other. This is happening in North America where the plate carrying the western part of California is slipping northward along the San Andreas fault.

In other places, such as Japan and the west of South America, two plates are pushing against each other and one is forced to dive deep into the Earth. In yet other places, such as Iceland and the Red Sea, two plates are moving apart and the gap between them is being filled with basalt lava from volcanoes.

▽ *This picture from space shows part of Arabia at the top and Africa at the bottom. In the past Arabia and Africa were joined together. They were split when earthquakes opened up a rift between them.*

◁ *This young Australian koala was born tiny and helpless. It climbed into its mother's pouch and then stayed there for about six months before setting off on its own. Animals such as koalas that rear their young in pouches are called marsupials. Early marsupials lived on a piece of continent that later split into three smaller pieces. These are now Antarctica, South America and Australia. The marsupials in Antarctica died of cold. Most of those in South America were killed by other animals that crossed from North America. But those in Australia survived.*

As earthquake waves travel through the Earth they are changed by the layers they pass through. So by recording distant earthquakes with seismographs, scientists have been able to work out how thick the plates are and what lies beneath them.

Earth's plates

The plates are usually about 60 miles thick and they lie on top of a layer where the rock is molten or nearly molten. The plates slip on this layer, rather as a mat slips on a wet floor. The molten or nearly molten rock beneath the plates seems to be where the basalt lava poured out by volcanoes comes from.

When two plates slowly move apart, the hot molten rock or magma wells up to fill the gap and new plate material is formed. Some of the magma overflows at the surface as basalt lava. Above the lava, seawater floods in to fill the top part of the gap. This is the way the Earth's oceans have formed.

The longer an ocean has been growing, the wider it is. The Red Sea between Africa and Arabia has only been growing for about 10 million years so it is quite narrow. The South Atlantic and Indian Oceans are much wider because they have been growing for about 200 million years.

How the Earth used to look

Because the South Atlantic and Indian Oceans were not there 200 million years ago, you can imagine what the Earth looked like at that time by squashing these two oceans up until they vanish. If you do this, you can see how the continents of South America, Africa, India, Australia, and Antarctica all fitted together. North America and Asia also fitted on, so at that time there was only one very big continent in the world.

The dinosaurs and other animals of 200 million years ago could roam freely over much of the vast continent. Then it started to split up, bit by bit. As the pieces of continent moved apart, the animals and plants were split up into groups, each group on its own piece of continent. Over millions of years, the groups of animals on the cut-off pieces of continent evolved in their own special way.

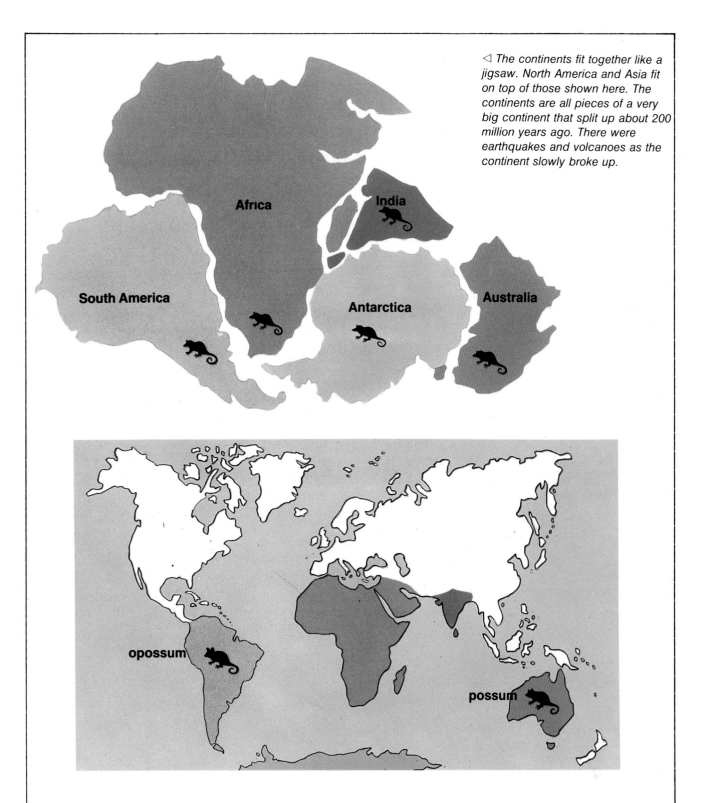

◁ *The continents fit together like a jigsaw. North America and Asia fit on top of those shown here. The continents are all pieces of a very big continent that split up about 200 million years ago. There were earthquakes and volcanoes as the continent slowly broke up.*

△ *The pieces of continent now form the map we know today. They are still moving several inches each year. The gaps between them have been filled with layers of basalt lava from volcanoes. These layers form the ocean floor. On the moving continents plants and animals slowly changed. In South America some of the early marsupials slowly changed into opossums, in Australia they changed into possums.*

Mountain building

The continents sometimes bump into each other as they are carried around by the Earth's moving plates. When this happens the first places to feel the effects are the areas of sea floor surrounding the continents. These areas are often covered with layers of sedimentary rock. The layers get squeezed, thrust over each other and pushed upward to form mountains.

This is what happened when Africa was pushed against Europe to form the Alpine mountain belt, and when India was pushed against the rest of Asia to form the Himalayas. In other parts of the world, mountain belts with volcanoes have formed where the moving plates have carried an old ocean floor beneath a continent. The Andes mountains formed in this way.

▽ *The Dolomites in Italy are part of the Alpine mountain belt. The mountains began as layers of rock formed from shells, sands and clays on the sea floor. As Africa was pushed against Europe, the layers were squeezed and pushed upward.*

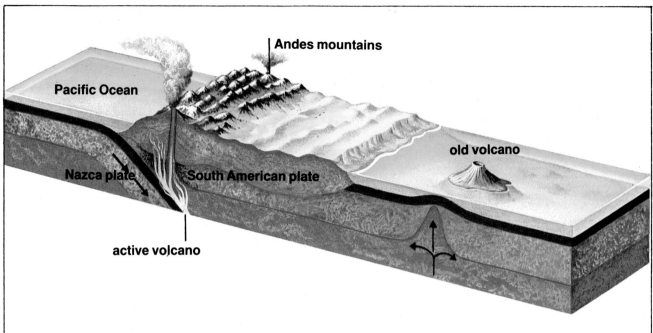

Andes mountains

Pacific Ocean

Nazca plate

South American plate

old volcano

active volcano

△ *Sometimes mountains are formed when a plate with an ocean on top pushes against a plate with a continent on top. This is happening beneath South America. The old*

ocean floor is forced to dive beneath the continent into the hot inner part of the Earth. It melts and the hot magma rises to form plutonic rocks such as granite or volcanoes. The land is

pushed up into a belt of mountains, called the Andes, which are shown below. ▽

△ *Folded layers of rock in the Pyrenees mountains, France. When rocks are heated and squeezed for millions of years, instead of breaking, the layers bend easily and fold like sheets of paper.*

△ *This piece of gneiss from Scotland was deposited as sediments on the sea floor about 3,000 million years ago. During mountain building, the rock was heated and squeezed. Quartz and feldspar crystals grew in the rock and formed pale colored bands. The rock was then squeezed even more and the bands were folded.*

When two plates push against each other to form a belt of mountains, the rocks below are heated and squeezed. Unlike cold rocks which break, hot rocks bend when they are squeezed. So if the heating and squeezing carries on for millions of years the layers of rock will bend and fold.

Heat and pressure changes rocks

The heat and pressure may also change the layers of rock in other ways. If the rock is a shale, tiny flakes of mica may grow in it and turn it into a slate. The tiny flakes all line up in the same plane, like the pages of a book. So if you hammer slate, it splits into very flat pieces. Such pieces of slate make very good roofs for houses. With further heating and squeezing, the mica flakes get bigger and crystals of other minerals may grow in the rock.

Sometimes beautiful red crystals of garnet are formed. Quartz and feldspar crystals may separate into pale colored bands. Such a rock is called a gneiss, which is pronounced "nice." In the end, the rock may get so hot that the quartz and feldspar start to melt and magma is formed.

How old is the Earth?

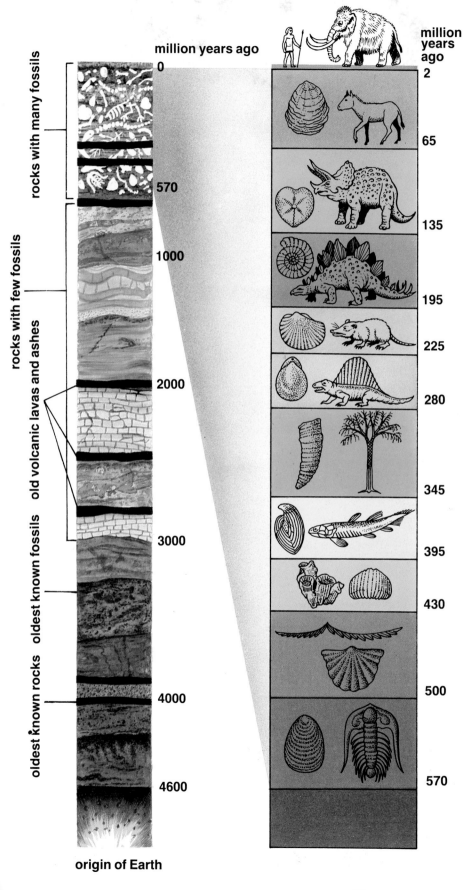

million years ago

million years ago

0

2

65

570

135

1000

195

225

2000

280

345

3000

395

430

4000

500

4600

570

rocks with many fossils

rocks with few fossils

old volcanic lavas and ashes

oldest known fossils

oldest known rocks

origin of Earth

◁ On the Earth's continents there are thick piles of layered rocks. The youngest layers are at the top, further down they get older and older. Some of the rocks are lavas or ashes from old volcanoes. Others are sedimentary rocks such as limestone, sandstone and shale.

Scientists use machines called mass spectrometers to find out how long ago the volcanic rocks cooled. The ages of the other layers can then be worked out using these dates. The rocks at the bottom formed not long after the formation of the Earth. Here there are no remains of past life. Traces of tiny living things first appear in the layers above, and near the top a layer with many fossil shells suddenly appears.

Scientists have carefully drawn and studied all the fossils in this layer and those above. They have given each layer a name, depending on its fossils. The first layer with many fossils is called the Cambrian layer. The bottom of this layer is about 570 million years old. All the fossils in it lived in the sea. There are animals rather like giant cockroaches, called trilobites, and shells of creatures like oysters, called brachiopods. The layers above all have different fossils and different names.

Scientists use machines called mass spectrometers to find out how long ago rocks that were once molten, cooled. The oldest rocks so far come from space. Some are rocks from the Moon brought back by astronauts. Some are lumps called meteorites that have crashed into the Earth by accident.

The origins of the Earth

The oldest Moon rocks and meteorites all cooled about 4,600 million years ago. Scientists think that the Sun, the Earth, the Moon, other planets and meteorites all formed just before this time, from a vast spinning disc of dust and gas. The Sun formed from the center of the disc while the Earth and other bodies formed from the outer part of it. The comets we sometimes see shooting past Earth may be left-over clumps of this dust and gas.

Many scientists think that the dust and gas that later formed the Earth, Moon and other big planets first collected into little planets. These little planets were probably less than 180 miles in diameter. It seems that some of the little planets stayed as the bodies we now call asteroids. Others smashed into each other and broke into pieces, some of which crashed into the Earth as meteorites.

Most of the little planets were pulled together by gravity to form large bodies such as the Earth and Moon. The large bodies got very hot and some of them, such as the Earth, melted and separated into different layers. The heaviest materials, such as iron, sank to the center while the lighter materials, such as granite and gases, rose to the surface.

After the large bodies such as the Earth were formed, little planets and giant meteorites continued to crash into them, leaving vast craters behind. On the Earth, all these early craters have long since worn away.

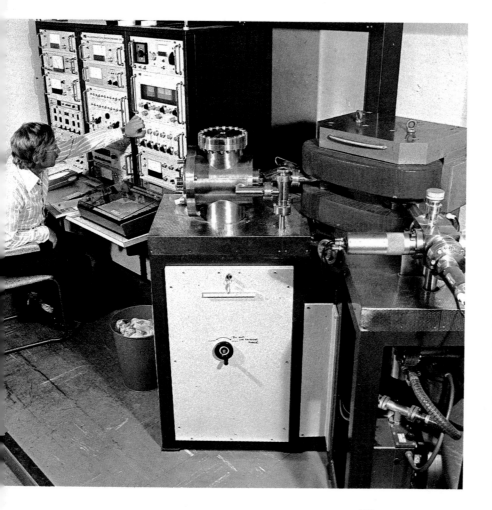

◁ This machine is a mass spectrometer, used to find out how long ago rocks that were once molten cooled.

Samples of rock are ground into powder, and then placed in the mass spectrometer. The machine then produces lots of numbers from which scientists work out when the rock cooled.

As well as volcanic and plutonic rocks, the machines are used to tell how long ago rocks such as gneisses cooled. Because gneisses formed during mountain building long ago, scientists can work out the ages of the old, now flattened, mountain ranges.

▷ Comets, like Halley's comet shown here, are made of dust and ice. They were probably left over after the Sun, Earth and other planets formed from a spinning cloud of gas, dust and ice about 4,600 million years ago.

▽ The Moon's surface is very old compared with that of the Earth. The craters show where giant meteorites hit the Moon soon after the Moon and Earth formed about 4,600 million years ago. Meteorites like these must also have hit Earth.

Inside the Earth

It is not easy to find out about the layers of rock deep inside the Earth. One way is to drill holes into the crust and bring up bits of rock to look at. Another way is to look carefully at the lumps of rock brought up by volcanoes. Some of these lumps seem to come from the thick layer below the crust called the mantle.

To find out further about the layers inside the Earth, scientists make use of earthquakes. Quakes in places such as Japan or New Zealand can be recorded by seismographs on the other side of the world, such as Scotland. As the shock waves travel through the Earth, they are changed by the different layers they pass through. The changes in the waves tell scientists something about these different layers.

▽ *Earthquake waves show that the Earth is layered like an onion. Beneath the thin outer crust is a thick layer of hot rock called the mantle. The crust and the outer part of the mantle together form the plates. These slip on a layer of partly molten rock within the mantle. Beneath the mantle is a very hot metal core.*

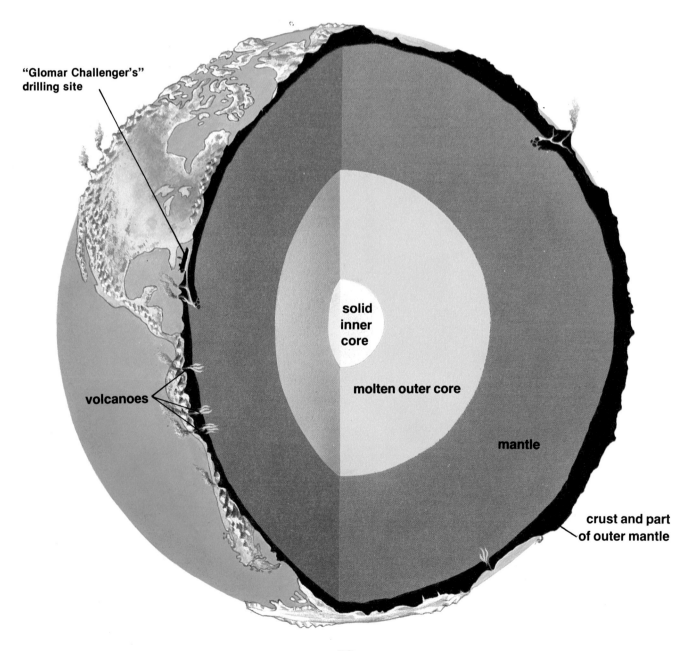

"Glomar Challenger's" drilling site

volcanoes

solid inner core

molten outer core

mantle

crust and part of outer mantle

◁ Ships like this drill deep holes in the ocean floor to find out more about the Earth's crust. The rocks that are brought up show that the top layer of ocean crust is mostly made of tiny shells. Beneath is a layer of basalt lavas and at the bottom is a layer of dark rock with big crystals. The crust beneath the oceans is about three miles thick, much thinner than the crust below the continents.

▽ The green bit in the top right hand corner of this lump of basalt lava is a piece of the Earth's mantle. The green color comes from the mineral olivine. As magma from the mantle rises up a crack, it sometimes tears off lumps of green mantle rock.

△ This iron and nickel meteorite gives us an idea of what the Earth's core may be made of. It probably came from the center of a small planet which broke up in space. Before it broke up, the planet melted and an iron and nickel core separated out.

By measuring changes in shock waves from earthquakes scientists have worked out the thickness of the Earth's crust beneath the continents. The thickness varies from place to place. Beneath mountain ranges such as the Alps and Andes the crust is up to 36 miles thick. In these places two plates have pushed together and caused the crust to thicken.

The continental crust is thinnest at the edges of some continents such as the west coast of Africa and the east coast of North America. The edges of these continents thinned as they moved apart when the Atlantic Ocean was formed. At these edges the continental crust is so thin that it lies below sea level.

Continental shelves

The thin edges of the continents that lie below sea level are called the continental shelves. They are often covered with layers of shale, sandstone and limestone, less than 200 million years old. Pools of oil and gas have often been found in the sandstone and limestone layers. The oil and gas is sometimes found trapped beneath a folded layer of shale or in a fossil coral reef in limestone.

Pools of oil and gas like this were formed from the bodies of tiny sea creatures that piled up on an ancient sea floor. The bodies were squashed by the weight of the sediments above and after millions of years they turned into oil and gas. Because oil and gas are lighter than water or rocks, they moved upward toward the surface, until they were trapped.

Ancient rocks

Toward the centers of the continents the rocks often get older and older. Scientists have found that many of them are more than about 2000 million years old. There is no oil in these very old rocks, but they often contain valuable metals such as gold or useful ones such as iron. The gold is found in cracks in granites and as tiny particles in ancient river beds. The iron is often found in layered rocks called banded ironstones.

Many of the very old rocks in the heart of the continents are quite different from younger ones. Among them are rocks very like the oldest rocks on the Moon.

◁ These scientists are looking at cores of rock brought up from a bore hole. Cores like this show what the top layer of crust below the continents is made of. Granite is the most common rock but there are volcanic rocks and sedimentary ones such as limestone, sandstone and shale as well. There are also rocks such as gneiss which have been squeezed and heated during mountain building. The bottom layers of the crust are probably made up of dark rocks with big crystals. Earthquake waves show that the continental crust is up to 36 miles thick beneath some mountains.

The Earth's magnetism

As well as gravity, the Earth has another invisible force called magnetism. But while everything on the Earth including ourselves, feels the Earth's gravity, only some things feel the Earth's magnetism. Lumps of iron and the mineral magnetite, which is made of iron and oxygen, feel the Earth's magnetism. Both iron and magnetite can be made into objects called magnets.

Magnets

Magnets always have two ends, one called the north-seeking magnetic pole and the other called the south-seeking magnetic pole. The north-seeking magnetic pole is pulled toward the Earth's north magnetic pole, which lies in northern Canada. The south-seeking magnetic pole is pulled toward the Earth's south magnetic pole, which lies near the coast of Antarctica.

If you were a magnet, your head might be your north magnetic pole and your feet would then be your south magnetic pole. It would be difficult to stand or walk because your head would always be pulled one way and your feet would always be pulled one way and your feet the other. It would be even more difficult to swim because your head would always be pulled toward the Earth's magnetic north pole.

Animals use the Earth's magnetism

Fortunately our bodies are not magnets and we do not feel the Earth's magnetism in the same way we feel its gravity. But some birds and animals do sense the Earth's magnetism and use it to find their way around. Pigeons, gulls and robins all use it to help them find the right direction to fly.

Long ago, sailors also learned how to use the Earth's magnetism to find their way in cloudy weather. When the night sky was clear they could find the direction by looking for the North Star. The North Star always shows the direction of north. But when the sky was cloudy, the early sailors often lost their way.

Then they learned to make compasses by stroking an iron needle with a lump of magnetite. This turned the needle into a magnet so that one end of the needle always pointed toward the Earth's north magnetic pole.

◁ Sailors use magnetic compasses to help them steer ships. The compass needle always points to the Earth's north magnetic pole.

The Earth's magnetism is like that of a giant magnet. If you place a piece of paper on top of a small magnet and then shake some iron filings onto the paper, the filings will become very excited.

Some will rush toward one end of the magnet and point toward its north-seeking magnetic pole. Some will rush to the magnet's other end and point to its south-seeking magnetic pole. Some will stay where they are, but they will still line up so that each end points to one of the magnetic poles of the magnet.

If you imagine that the magnet is a huge magnet inside the Earth, you can see how the Earth's magnetism swings compass needles around just as the magnet swings the iron filings around.

▷ *The Northern lights shown here are caused by the Earth's magnetism. The Earth's magnetism stretches far out into space. It affects the tiny particles which are always streaming away from the Sun. These tiny particles carry electricity, just as wire does when you connect its two ends up to the terminals of a battery.*

When an electric current flows along a wire, the wire becomes magnetized. It produces its own magnetism and also feels the force of Earth's magnetism. This force causes the wire to move slightly. The same thing happens to the tiny particles from the Sun as they speed toward Earth. The Earth's magnetism causes them to change direction slightly. Some of them move toward the Earth's north magnetic pole and others to the Earth's south magnetic pole.

When they reach the top of the atmosphere near the magnetic poles, they hit the tiny particles of nitrogen and oxygen in the air. The tiny particles of nitrogen and oxygen then give off colored lights. These beautiful lights can only be seen in belts around the Earth's magnetic poles.

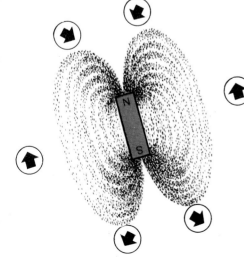

◁▷ *The Earth's magnetism is rather like that of a huge magnet, with its north magnetic pole beneath northern Canada. A compass needle on the surface of the Earth here will try to point downward. Near the south magnetic pole, which is below the coast of Antarctica, a compass needle will try to point upward. Over the rest of the Earth, compass needles always try to point in the directions shown.*

Make your own compass!

1, 2, 3, 4...
9, 10, 11, 12...
17, 18, 19, 20.

Stroking the same way each time, stroke a needle with a magnet at least 20 times.

Cut off the top of a cork and then stick the needle through the flat piece of cork.

Float the cork in water. The needle will point to Earth's north magnetic pole.

Metals and minerals

Today we use more different metals and minerals than ever before. New sources of useful metals such as iron, copper, aluminum and tin or sources of energy such as oil and coal are always needed. So scientists have worked out lots of methods for finding these sources.

One method is to take pictures of the ground. For many years they have taken photographs of the ground from aircraft to help in the search. Now they also use pictures taken from satellites in space. The satellites have cameras which take pictures of large areas of the Earth. The pictures are sent by radio waves to special stations on the ground.

The pictures show faults and folds in layers of rock as well as different soils and plants. From these clues scientists can tell where new sources of metals and minerals are likely to be.

▽ *This picture shows the Baluchistan desert in Asia. It was taken by a satellite about 600 miles above the Earth's surface and covers a distance of about 120 miles from top to bottom. The ridges at the top are rock layers that have been pushed upright during mountain building. Scientists used the picture to find a new source of copper just below the ridges at the top.*

Scientists also use the Earth's magnetism to help them find sources of some metals, such as iron and chromium. Some sources of these metals have their own magnetism. If you carry a compass over the ground near one of them, the compass needle will move.

Using magnetism to find metals

The magnetism of the metal source tugs at the compass needle so it no longer points toward the Earth's north magnetic pole. As you move away from the metal source, the compass needle will move back and will again point to the Earth's north magnetic pole. You can see how this works for yourself by using a compass to find things made from iron or steel which somebody has hidden under a carpet or mat. When scientists search for these sources of metals they use instruments rather like very sensitive compasses to detect small changes in the Earth's magnetism.

Scientists also use earthquake waves, radio waves, electric currents and other methods to help them in their search for new sources of metals. When they find a promising place, they go there and break the rocks open with a hammer to see if the minerals they are looking for are really there.

△ A scientist breaks rocks with a hammer to see if minerals containing useful metals are inside. If he finds enough of any mineral, it may be worth starting up a mine.

◁ This man is checking a machine which measures earth waves. The heavy trucks beside him shake the ground setting off waves which travel down into the rocks beneath. If they hit a layer of different rock, some of the waves bounce back and are recorded by detectors at the surface. The waves show where layers that contain oil may be.

▷ Metal detectors buzz when a piece of buried metal is nearby. The detector uses invisible waves rather like radio waves to search for metal. Scientists sometimes use detectors rather like this to show where new sources of metals may be.

▷ Stream beds are good places to look for tiny bits of gold or tin ore. The heavy gold or black tin ore stays in the pan while the lighter bits of rock are washed away. When gold or black tin ore is found like this, the source of the metal is likely to be farther up the stream. The source may turn out to be cracks in granite which have later filled with gold or tin ore.

Mining the Earth's riches

After careful searching, scientists sometimes find sources of metals or minerals that are large enough to be worth mining. The metals or minerals occur in many different kinds of rock or soil.

Metals are not often found by themselves, they are usually in minerals called ores which also contain oxygen, sulphur, silicon, or other substances. Iron ore often occurs as layers in sedimentary rocks, such as the very old banded ironstones. Copper ore is often found close to old, worn away volcanoes. Tin ore occurs in granites and stream beds.

Gemstones

Gemstones such as diamonds and opals are much rarer than metal ores. Diamonds are found in the pipes of old volcanoes which instead of hot lava emitted a very rare kind of cold powdery rock with lots of olivine crystals in it. Diamonds are made of ordinary carbon, just like soot or coke. To make diamonds, the carbon was squeezed by the high pressure in the Earth's mantle, about 60 miles below the surface. The squeezing forced the tiny particles of carbon close together to form diamonds. The diamonds were then carried up to the Earth's surface by a mixture of gas and olivine crystals from the mantle layer.

Opals are often found in cracks in sedimentary rocks and are made of the same materials as quartz together with water. An opal is made up of millions and millions of tiny balls of these materials. These scatter the light to give all the colors of the rainbow, just as raindrops scatter sunlight to give rainbows.

△ This miner is working in an underground opal mine in Australia. To remove minerals that are far below the surface, miners have to sink deep holes and then tunnel sideways.

◁ Dredging for tin ore in Malaysia. The ore was washed down to here by rivers from granite mountains nearby. Tin ore and sand are carried up to the dredge by a chain of buckets. On the dredge, the unwanted sand is separated from the tin ore.

After scientists have found metal ores or other minerals worth mining, miners work out the best way of getting the material out of the ground. Oil or gas is usually easy to remove. A deep hole is drilled down to the pool of oil or gas and lined with a steel pipe. The weight of the rocks above squeezes the oil or gas and forces it up the pipe to the surface.

Minerals that are close to the surface are also easy to get at. They are often removed by digging machines and then put on a moving belt that carries them away to be treated. The most difficult minerals to get are those that are far below the surface. Miners have to sink deep holes and then tunnel sideways until they reach the mineral. The rock is broken up with picks or digging machines or sometimes with explosives. The mineral is carried away on trucks or moving belts and lifted to the surface.

△ Production platforms like this are used to extract oil and gas from deep below the seabed. On the platform gas and water are separated from the oil. The oil is then pumped to land through a strong steel pipeline. Once on land it is taken to a refinery where gasoline is made from it.

▷ This is an iron ore mine in Australia. The iron ore comes from hills made of a very old sedimentary rock called banded ironstone. The rock with ore is broken up and the ore is placed on moving belts which carry it away to be stored in piles. Trucks take the ore to a port where it is loaded onto large ships. The ships then carry the ore to places where iron and steel are made.

▷ The iron ore is heated with coke and limestone in a blast furnace. A blast of hot gases removes oxygen from the ore and turns it into iron. The hot molten iron is poured into molds. Most iron is used to make a tough form of iron called steel. The iron is heated again in another furnace where impurities are removed and steel is made.

After miners have dug metal ore out of the ground, it is taken to a factory where the metal is separated from the rest of the ore.

This is usually done by heating the ore with carbon in the form of coke. The tiny particles of carbon join up with the tiny particles of oxygen in the ore to form carbon dioxide gas. The gas escapes and the tiny particles of metal are left on their own as hot liquid metal. The hot liquid is poured into molds and cools into solid blocks of metal.

Metal sheets and molded metal

Many different things can be done with the metal blocks to make them more useful. Sometimes they are squeezed between rollers, again and again, until the blocks have been flattened out into thin metal sheets. Sometimes they are heated until they are slightly soft and then hammered into the shape that is needed. Sometimes they are heated until they melt again and can be poured into molds to give them the right shape.

Metals are very useful for making things because they are strong, and they can stand high temperatures without burning, softening or melting. The different metals are used to make different things. See how many different metals are used in your kitchen or in a car. A magnet would help you tell the metals apart. It will be attracted to iron and most kinds of steel but not to other metals such as aluminum, zinc or stainless steel.

Reusing metal

Most metals can be used again and again. When something made of metal has worn out, it can be taken to a scrap yard where the different metals it contains are sorted out. Each metal is then taken to a different factory and heated until it melts. The liquid metal is poured into molds and used in the same way as new metal.

◁ When cars and other objects made of metal are worn out, the metals can be used again. Cars are made of many different metals. Their bodies are usually made of steel sheet and much of the engine is made of solid iron. Copper, lead, zinc, aluminum, tin, chromium, nickel and other metals are also used in cars. These metals can often be separated out and used again.

Index

1 2 3 4 5 6 7 8 9 10—WZ—90 89 88 87 86 85